Alibi

Kristin Butcher

Orca currents

ORCA BOOK PUBLISHERS

Library and Archives Canada Cataloguing in Publication

Butcher, Kristin, author
Alibi / Kristin Butcher.
(Orca currents)

Issued in print and electronic formats.
ISBN 978-1-4598-0767-9 (pbk.).--ISBN 978-1-4598-0768-6 (bound)
ISBN 978-1-4598-0769-3 (pdf).--ISBN 978-1-4598-0770-9 (epub)

I. Title. II. Series: Orca currents
PS8553.U6972A45 2014   jc813'.54   C2014-901590-9

First published in the United States, 2014
Library of Congress Control Number: 2014935393

Summary: Christine wants to help her aunt by catching the thief
who has been targeting a small tourist town.

MIX
Paper from
responsible sources
FSC® C016245
www.fsc.org

*Orca Book Publishers is dedicated to preserving the environment and has
printed this book on Forest Stewardship Council® certified paper.*

Orca Book Publishers gratefully acknowledges the support for its
publishing programs provided by the following agencies: the Government
of Canada through the Canada Book Fund and the Canada Council for the Arts,
and the Province of British Columbia through the BC Arts Council
and the Book Publishing Tax Credit.

Cover photography by Getty Images
Author photo by Lisa Pederson Photography

ORCA BOOK PUBLISHERS   ORCA BOOK PUBLISHERS
PO Box 5626, Stn. B   PO Box 468
Victoria, BC Canada   Custer, WA USA
V8R 6S4   98240-0468

www.orcabook.com
Printed and bound in Canada.

17 16 15 14 • 4 3 2 1

For my River Writer cohorts—
an indispensable posse of beta readers

Chapter One

Aunt Maude is standing on the station platform. Even though it's been two years since I've seen her, she hasn't changed a bit—except for her glasses. The hot-pink frames are new. She pushes them up the bridge of her nose, but right away they slide down again.

I smile and wave from the bus. She grins and waves back.

Already I'm excited. I have no idea what Aunt Maude has planned for us, but I know it will be good. It always is. Aunt Maude lives by a different set of rules than other adults. When I was nine, she took me to a horror movie and told my mom it was a Disney film. When I was eleven, she taught me to play poker—for money. On my thirteenth birthday, she took me makeup shopping and didn't try to talk me out of purple lipstick and glittery black polish.

Though I call her Aunt Maude, she's actually my mom's aunt. That makes her my great-aunt. And she really is. Great, I mean. Normally, I wouldn't consider hanging out with a seventy-one-year-old lady for an afternoon, never mind a couple weeks of my summer vacation. But when Aunt Maude invited me to Witcombe for a visit, I jumped at the chance. Why wouldn't I? I have more

fun with her than I do with most of
my friends.

"Christine!" I'm barely off the bus
when she swallows me in a fierce hug
that takes my breath away.

"Aunt Maude," I gasp when she
releases me. "It's good to see you."

"And you, my girl. It's been far too
long." She throws an arm around my
shoulder and squeezes again. My bones
fuse. Old ladies aren't supposed to be
that strong.

"There's my bag." I squirm free and
make a dive for it.

"Just the one?" Aunt Maude says.

"And my backpack," I tell her,
swinging it onto my shoulder.

"Well, then, let's be off." She laughs
and leads the way to the exit.

Aunt Maude owns an antique shop
in downtown Witcombe and lives in the
apartment above it. Since it's a sunny

day and the shop is only a couple of blocks from the bus station, we walk.

Though I've visited Witcombe before, I still gawk at everything like I'm a tourist. The town is caught in a time bubble. It's barely changed at all in 150 years. Oh sure, there are roads and cars and electricity, but there are also wooden sidewalks, hitching posts and old storefronts. On Main Street there's an ancient red telephone booth. And it works! The mailbox in front of the post office is old-fashioned too. Of course, there are restaurants, drugstores, banks and clothing stores like in big cities, but Witcombe businesses have to be one-of-a-kind. It's a law. You won't find any fast-food chains or big-box stores here.

You'd think that might discourage visitors, but it doesn't. The town buzzes with tourists all year long. There are cottagers in the summer and skiers in the winter.

Aunt Maude has lived in Witcombe her whole life. As soon as we step out of the bus station, she waves to a man in a plaid shirt and a ballcap. "Afternoon, George. The pipes have quieted right down."

The man smiles. "Glad I could help."

"Plumber," Aunt Maude tells me. "The hot-water pipes were rattling something fierce last week. In twenty minutes George had them hushed right up. He's a genius with a wrench." And then she greets the next person. It goes on like that the whole way to the antique shop.

Aunt Maude fishes a key out of her pocket and sticks it into the lock. "Darn thing," she fumes after fighting with it for several seconds. "It's been giving me nothing but grief lately."

"Here. Let me try," I say, taking the skeleton key from her. "This is pretty old, Aunt Maude. Maybe it's time for a new lock."

She waves away my words. "Nonsense. The lock came with the door, and I don't have any intention of replacing either of them."

"But it must be easy to pick. Aren't you afraid of getting robbed?"

"Why would I be? I've had this shop for over thirty-five years, and in all that time I've never had so much as a teaspoon go missing. Besides, if I can't get the door open with the key, what makes you think a thief will have better luck without one?"

I ignore the sarcasm and say, "On the bus I was listening to the news, and they said there have been a bunch of burglaries in the area."

Finally, the key twists in the lock. I hand it back to Aunt Maude.

"That's in other towns," she says, turning the brass knob. "Not here in Witcombe."

I know better than to argue. Aunt Maude may be a free spirit, but she is also very stubborn. Pulling my suitcase behind me, I follow her inside and shut the door.

"Do you want the sign flipped to *OPEN?*" I ask.

"Yes, please," she says. "It's only 4:30. We have lots of time before we have to get ready for the tour."

"What tour?"

Aunt Maude's eyes suddenly look like they're being held open with toothpicks, and her voice gets all spooky. "The ghost walk."

I feel my eyebrows shoot up. "What's that?"

She grins. "Something new—I think you'll like it. The idea came to me last week. All day long tourists come into the shop, and while they're browsing, I tell them stories about Witcombe. I tell

them about Old Joe Miner, the legend of Wheaton's Bridge, the mystery of the abandoned mill and all the other town stories. So I got to thinking, why not show people the places that go with the tales? It will be interesting for them and fun for me. Tonight is the first tour. You wouldn't believe how many people have signed up."

"Ghost walk, huh? Sounds interesting. But are there really ghosts in Witcombe?"

She shrugs and smiles mysteriously. "I guess we'll find out, won't we?"

Chapter Two

At 8:45 Aunt Maude and I climb the
stairs of the gazebo in the park. There
are already two people waiting, and Aunt
Maude checks them off her list. During
the next fifteen minutes, the rest of the
tour group trickles in. By 9:00, there's
quite a gang—eleven, not counting Aunt
Maude and me. Lucky thirteen, I think—
perfect for a ghost walk.

The sun has already slipped behind the mountains, and though the sky is still blue, the color is leaking out of it fast. Aunt Maude doesn't waste any time getting started. She spreads her arms and twirls in the middle of the gazebo.

"This gazebo, ladies and gentlemen, is the heart of Witcombe. It is the oldest structure in the town. It was the first structure to go up, even before the church or any of the houses. That's right. The founders of the town—Bruno Wittier and Jeremiah Lancombe—lived out of the back of their wagons while they built this gazebo. Of course, the deck and roof have been replaced many times, and the gazebo's had more coats of paint than people can count, but otherwise it's the same as it ever was. The timber came from the trees in the area, and the gingerbread trim is all handmade." She runs a hand down one of the columns. "That's what I call craftsmanship.

"While the rest of the town was being built, the gazebo was the center of things. That's why it was made round. It symbolized the unbroken circle of community that Wittier and Lancombe wanted Witcombe to become. This was where people shared their suppers, held their first town meetings, celebrated holidays and campaigned for political office." Aunt Maude smiles and sighs dreamily. "More than a few young ladies have received marriage proposals here too."

She leads us down the steps and around the side of the gazebo to a shiny metal plaque. "*Witcombe Gazebo— erected in 1862 for the citizens of Witcombe, British Columbia. May friends and neighbors always find each other here.*" She allows the words to sink in before continuing.

"Imagine the tales this old gazebo could tell—the secrets it knows, the wishes

it's heard." Her voice becomes quiet— almost a whisper. "It is said that at night when the town is asleep, the gazebo relives the past. Sometimes it's a band concert. Sometimes a May Day picnic or a summer dance. It might merely be children playing hide-and-seek. Always happy times though. And if folks waken and hear the commotion, they fall back to sleep smiling."

"Oh, my. That sounds lovely," says an elderly, white-haired woman beside me. I hadn't noticed her until now—probably because she's so short. She barely comes to my shoulder. "I wouldn't mind being haunted like that," she adds with a sigh.

"Well then, we'll have to keep our ears open tonight, sister," says the woman standing beside her. "Maybe we could join the fun."

As everyone chuckles, I blink. It's like I'm seeing double. The second old

lady is exactly like the first, right down to the clothes, earrings and hairdo. These two women are absolutely identical. They even have the same wrinkles. I blink a couple more times. Maybe it's my eyes. I glance around the group and then back to the old ladies. Nope. There's only one of everybody else, and there are two of them.

I must be wearing my confusion on my face, because the woman closest to me pats my arm. "It's all right, dear. It happens all the time. We're twins. We have been our whole lives." She laughs at her own joke.

Her sister clucks her tongue and shakes her head. "Oh, Agatha, you are such a kidder. Stop teasing the poor girl." She sticks out her hand. "How do you do. I'm Hilary Spence. And this is my sister, Agatha. We're on holiday. We're staying in one of those lovely lakefront cottages on Cedar Road.

This is such a beautiful area. I don't know how we'll get to see everything in the few days we have, but we're certainly going to try. Isn't that right, sister?"

Agatha Spence nods and points to the group trailing after Aunt Maude. "It's very nice to chat, Hilary, but we're missing the tour. Come along."

An hour and a half into the ghost walk, Aunt Maude is still going strong. She knows exactly how to play her audience, amping up her stories to keep pace with the growing darkness. Cloaked in shadows cast by the antique streetlights, Witcombe is now eerie, and the group creeps forward in a nervous knot.

"Greeley House is our last stop," Aunt Maude announces as we start up a treed lane. "Or Greedy House, as it's known by the locals."

Though the street is well lit, the trees contort the light into unsettling shapes that follow us up the road. It's like

we're being stalked. At a pair of rusted wrought-iron gates, we stop.

"This is Greeley House," Aunt Maude says.

As one, we turn and look past the padlocked gates. The yard is overgrown with tall grass and unkempt shrubs. Beyond is a two-story mansion, equally unkempt. Moss has taken over the roof, and ivy has claimed the walls. The stairs to the front door are caved in with rot, and the windows are boarded up. The place looks like a teardown to me, but I can tell it was once a beautiful home.

"This house was built in 1922 by Simon Greeley. His father, Fred Greeley, was the town butcher. A kinder, more generous soul you could never hope to meet. Fred was exactly the sort of citizen Lancombe and Wittier had hoped would populate Witcombe. When he died, everyone thought his son would take over his butcher shop, but Simon

had no desire to follow in his father's footsteps. Simon sold the business and invested the money in the stock market. It was a foolish thing to do, but even fools get lucky sometimes, and Simon made millions from his investments.

"People expected he would take his money to the big city, but he surprised them again. Instead, he set out to buy Witcombe. He opened a savings and loan, offering incentives to lure customers away from the competition. Eventually, the other financial institution closed its doors, leaving only Simon's bank. The residents of Witcombe were at his mercy—except he had none. People took loans and mortgages at rates they couldn't repay, and as a result, they lost everything. The bank fore-closed on dozens of loans. Homeowners became renters. Businessmen became employees. And they all answered to Simon Greeley.

"Greeley House was Simon's *pièce de résistance*. It was his castle. His way of showing that he'd become king."

"So what happened?"

"In 1929 the stock market crashed," Aunt Maude replies. "Simon lost everything, and one night, in a drunken stupor, he fell down the stairs of his castle and died. The town took over the house for unpaid taxes. No one wanted to buy it, so they locked the gates and walked away. As you can see, the place is decaying. One day it will just fall down."

"Are there ghosts in it?" a woman asks.

Aunt Maude shrugs. "I wouldn't be surprised. From the stories I've heard, Simon Greeley would never have left his house. But nobody's been inside for over seventy-five years, so…" She shrugs and leaves her sentence hanging.

"If the town is waiting for it to collapse, why are the grounds lit up?"

I'm surprised—not by the question, but by the guy who asked it. He can't be more than a couple of years older than I am, and he's gorgeous. How did I not notice him before now? I do a quick head count. There are now fourteen of us.

"It's a reminder of the evils of greed," Aunt Maude says. "Witcombe almost came to ruin at Simon Greeley's hands. We don't want that to happen again."

"Speaking of greed," he says, "I just heard on the radio that there's been another robbery. Kaleden this time. Two customers in a convenience store had their pockets picked."

"The thief is getting closer," I say.

One of the Spence sisters gasps, though I have no idea which one. They should wear name tags. "That's terrible," she says. "Is no place safe? When did this happen?"

"About an hour ago."

That does it. Ghost walk forgotten, people start talking over one another about the ongoing spree of robberies. I glance around for the guy who gave us the news, but he's vanished.

And then I see him—at least, I think I do—beyond the tour group and padlocked gates, at the back of the mansion. But I can't be sure. In the time it takes me to blink, he disappears behind the house.

Chapter Three

I peer over my shoulder before slipping around the corner into Greeley Lane. There's that name again. I haven't even set foot on Simon Greeley's property yet, and already I feel like I'm trespassing. The morning is swimming in sunshine, but the street feels as eerie as it did last night.

I told Aunt Maude I was going for a run before the day got too warm. I didn't,

however, tell her where I planned to run. I also didn't tell her about the guy I saw sneaking around the back of the Greeley mansion. Not that I *won't* tell her. But I want to check things out first.

The situation is more than a little suspicious. The condemned house is surrounded by a wrought-iron fence that's clearly intended to keep people out. But this guy went through it like a hot knife through butter. He obviously knows his way around. How is that possible? He's not a local. Aunt Maude said she didn't know him.

I think maybe he's the thief, and he's hiding out in the mansion. Kaleden is only a forty-five-minute drive from Witcombe. According to the news report, the robberies at the convenience store happened around nine o'clock. That would give the thief plenty of time to get back here to join the tour. No one in the group saw him arrive, so he

could claim he'd been with us all along. It was an instant alibi.

I move cautiously up the road, half expecting bad guys to leap out from behind every tree. Talk about an overactive imagination.

When I reach the front of the house, I'm less than impressed. Cloaked in night shadows, the mansion was imposing and foreboding. Now, in the light of day, it's just tired and dilapidated. If I sneezed in its direction, it would probably fall down.

I grab the iron bars with both hands and shake them. They don't shake. There's not even a quiver. The fence may be nearly a hundred years old, but it's rock solid.

I glance down the road again and then start up the side of the property, along the fence line. The grass here has been trampled. Just beyond the house the path of crushed grass stops.

This must be where the guy entered the property.

I frown at the fence. This is going to be like breaking into Fort Knox. But this is where the guy went through. There must be a secret gate or something. As I step closer to examine it, I hear a noise—and freeze. It sounds like something heavy scraping across concrete. I look toward the house, but an overgrown hedge blocks my view. *Darn!* Still, if I can't see the person on the other side of the hedge, he can't see me either.

With that thought in mind, I search for a place to hide. Fortunately, there are trees and bushes everywhere, so I duck behind one.

I hide not a second too soon either. I've barely crouched down when out from the hedge comes the guy I saw sneaking around last night. He's whistling. I scrunch lower and peek through the leaves of the bush. When he

gets to the fence, he pulls down on one of the iron bars and lifts it out. *Aha!* Cute trick. I watch as he turns sideways and threads himself through the opening. As he replaces the bar, I make a mental note of which one it is.

Resuming his whistling, the guy starts jogging through the trampled grass toward the road. I scoot around to the other side of the bush. If he looks back, I don't want him to see me. But he's a man on a mission. When he reaches the street, he turns onto the sidewalk and keeps going.

When I'm sure he's gone, I creep out of my hiding place. Then I scamper soundlessly down the trampled path and peer along the road. All I see is the guy's back as he exits Greeley Lane onto the adjoining street.

Should I follow him? If he's the crook, chances are he's heading where there are lots of people. From what

I've heard and seen on television, pick-pockets like to work in crowds. That would be good for me too, because I could watch him without being seen. Who knows—I might actually catch him in the act.

I glance at Greeley House. With him gone, now is the perfect time to check out his hideaway. If he's stashed his loot in there, that's evidence.

It's a win-win situation. I opt for the house.

Even though I watched the guy work the fence, it stumps me at first, mostly because I reef on the wrong bar. Breaking and entering is new for me. Finally, I find the right iron picket. I grab it with both hands and yank hard. To my surprise, it comes away easily, leaving a half-inch gap where it's been cut. I pull the bar toward me and slide it out. Then I examine the fence where I removed the bar. At the base, a hole containing a

heavy-duty spring keeps the bar secure when it's in place. It's the same technique that's used to hold batteries inside a flashlight. I'm impressed. It's a pretty slick trick.

I climb through the opening in the fence and replace the bar. Then I scoot across the yard and slip behind the hedge. There's a wooden door. It's green, but weather and years of neglect have blistered the paint and warped the wood. That's probably why it scraped on the stone sill. That and the fact that the walkway is buckled. But if the guy could get the door open, so can I.

Anticipating resistance, I put my shoulder into it, turn the ancient knob and push. The noise that follows is so loud, I'm sure all of Witcombe must hear it. But I've come this far. There's no backing out now. Taking a deep breath, I leave the brilliant morning behind and venture into the darkness.

As I feel my way along the wall, I wonder why people didn't invest in windows back in the olden days. The damp plaster crumbles at my touch. Why didn't I think to bring a flashlight? Dank air invades my lungs and refuses to leave. I try breathing through my mouth, but now I can taste the rotting house as well as smell it.

I must be in a hallway, because I can see light ahead of me. I hurry toward it. The corridor gives way to a tiny cubicle with a window. It's small, and years of dirt are caked on the glass, but it provides enough daylight to see by.

The room is so tiny, a person with long arms could stand in the middle and touch the walls. But the guy is obviously living in it—well, sleeping anyway. There's an air mattress and sleeping bag on the floor and a backpack and a stack of clothing on a table. It's not exactly the Witcombe Hilton.

There is no other furniture, and no bags or boxes on the floor either. If the guy is the thief, he's storing his loot in another room. I head back to the hallway. I find a couple of doors, but they are locked and boarded up.

I head back to the exit. On a hook by the door is a flashlight.

"Fat lot of help you are now," I snort and walk outside. It's like surfacing in a lake after a long, deep dive. My lungs hungrily suck up the fresh air.

I'm still not convinced the guy is innocent, but I don't have any proof—yet. I guess I'll have to stake out the place again and follow him when he shows up.

I take a quick look around the grounds before slipping back through the fence and replacing the iron bar. No one will ever know I was here. I hurry back to the road. Why do I feel like I'm being watched?

Chapter Four

According to the thermometer hanging by the door, it's ninety-three degrees—and that's *inside* the antique shop. Aunt Maude's air-conditioning has packed it in. Talk about bad timing. We have set up fans all around the shop. If the electrical system doesn't blow a circuit, it will be a miracle.

The store is quiet. Aside from the occasional person running in from the street in the hope of cooling off for a few minutes, it's pretty dead. I've been put on dusting duty. In an antique shop, that's a never-ending job. Today the only items being dusted are the ones located near the fans.

"Christine!"

I jump and spin around. Aunt Maude is standing right behind me. I grab my chest and roll my eyes. "Are you trying to give me a heart attack or what? You shouldn't sneak up on a person like that."

She laughs. "I didn't sneak up on you. In fact, that's the third time I called your name. But your head is so close to that fan, you couldn't hear me."

"Oh." I shrug sheepishly. "I must've been dusting something underneath it."

That makes Aunt Maude laugh again. "The reason I was calling you was to give you the rest of the afternoon off.

It's sweltering in here. Besides, there aren't any customers. There's no point in both of us melting. Why don't you get your swimsuit and go for a dip in the community-center pool?"

"You should come too," I say. "Close the shop. You said it yourself—there are no customers. We could both go for a swim."

She pats my arm and prods me toward the stairs that lead to the apartment. "Don't you worry about me. I'll get my swim—in the bathtub this evening while you're making supper." Then she winks and gives me another push.

The community center is packed with people—swimmers and air-conditioning seekers. It is way too hot to be outside. I imagine there's hardly any room in the pool to swim, but simply submerging myself in the cool water will be a relief.

There are three pools—one for little kids and their parents, one with a water slide and a third, regulation-size pool complete with diving boards. That's the one I head for. Though this pool has no age restrictions, only proficient swimmers are allowed to use it. Even so, there are lifeguards all over the place, with fluorescent lime-green T-shirts and whistles around their necks. At my pool, three of them prowl the edges—a girl and two guys.

"Whoa!" One of them grabs the arm of a boy just before he rams into me. "You know the rules, Mason. No running on the pool deck. You'll hurt yourself or somebody else."

The boy hangs his head and nods.

The lifeguard ruffles the kid's hair and smiles. "Okay then. Try to remember from now on. Away you go." When the lifeguard turns to me, I see his face for the first time. It's the gorgeous guy

who's holed up in Greeley House. I'm sure my eyes bug out of my head.

"Sorry about that," he says and then adds with a shrug, "Kids. They don't mean to break the rules. They just forget."

I force a smile. "No problem." Then I carry on to the pool. *Whew!* He didn't recognize me. But I haven't taken two steps when his voice stops me again.

"Wait a second. Don't I know you?"

Rats! I paste a bewildered look on my face and turn around. "I don't think so."

He looks unsure for a couple of seconds. Then his expression clears, and a grin spreads across his features. "Sure, I do. Well, sort of. You were on that ghost walk last night, weren't you?"

I have to give the guy credit. He thinks fast. By reminding me I saw him on the ghost walk, he reinforces his alibi.

What can I say? I nod. "Right. You were the guy who told everyone about the thefts in Kaleden."

"Well, that's been the big news around here for the last week. There have been motel break-ins or pick-pocket robberies every day. From what I've heard, the police don't have a single suspect. They have no idea where the thief will strike next. Whoever's behind this is pretty clever."

Pat yourself on the back, why don't you? But, of course, I don't say that.

"It's only a matter of time before Witcombe gets hit."

Well, you'd know, I say to myself, but to him, I say, "I sure hope not."

"Hey, Simon," another lifeguard calls as he heads for us. "Coming to the barbecue at Abby's house?"

Simon? As in Simon Greeley? I know it's not the same guy, but could the name be more than a coincidence? Could this be a descendent of Simon Greeley?

Simon Lifeguard shakes his head. "No, man. I'd like to, but I can't. I'm whooped."

He checks his watch. "My shift is done in an hour, and then I gotta catch some z's."

Or perform another robbery.

I take this opportunity to sneak away. Yeah, I could still use a swim, but I have an hour before Simon is off-duty. I'll use that time to check out his digs once more. Maybe there's something in his backpack or buried beneath his pile of clothes. And if he's planning another theft, I can follow him.

The thing about air-conditioning is that it doesn't last. Within minutes of leaving the community center, I'm drenched in sweat. By the time I reach Greeley House, I'm sure I've sweated off five pounds. But there's no time to waste, so I run up the trampled trail, dislodge the iron bar, slip through the fence and race to the door.

At which point I stop.

The door to Greeley House is padlocked. Where did that come from? Simon's belongings are piled on the stone walkway in front of the door. And there's a notice nailed to the door—*PRIVATE PROPERTY. KEEP OUT. TRESPASSERS WILL BE PROSECUTED.*

Chapter Five

As I crouch behind a bush waiting for Simon Lifeguard to show up, I think about this new plot twist. It would seem I am not the only one who knows he has been hiding out in Greeley House. And now he's been evicted. I bet he wasn't planning on that.

I have no idea what time it is, but it feels like sweat has been trickling down

my back and puddling behind my knees for a couple of hours. The longer I wait, the more I start to think that Simon isn't going to show. Maybe his story about needing sleep was a lie. Maybe he had no intention of coming back here, or maybe he needed an excuse to skip the barbecue. What an idiot I am! Simon is probably committing another theft right this minute.

And instead of catching him in the act, I'm hiding behind a stupid bush, getting sunstroke. But I can't leave. The only way out is down Greeley Lane. If Simon shows up as I'm leaving, he'll see me for sure.

I wish I had brought my phone. If nothing else, I could pass the time on the Internet. I no sooner think this than I hear whistling. It must be Simon. I make myself as small as I can.

The bush I'm hiding behind is at the top of the trampled trail, near the

removable picket. I see Simon as soon as he leaves the sidewalk and starts up the side of the property. He could probably see me too if he was looking, but his gaze seems focused on his feet.

He lets himself through the fence and disappears behind the hedge. For a couple of seconds it's dead quiet. I picture the confused expression on his face when he sees the padlocked door and his belongings stacked in front of it. And then, as his brain finally figures out what has happened—

I don't have to use my imagination anymore. He lets loose with every swear-word I've ever heard—plus a few more. The guy is definitely upset. He emerges from behind the hedge, kicks at the grass, stomps back and forth and launches into another round of cursing. More grass kicking. More stomping. More swearing.

His antics remind me of a spoiled little boy who has been told he can't

have candy. He is so out of control it's funny, and, forgetting that I'm in hiding, I laugh.

I clap a hand over my mouth, but it's too late. He stops pacing and ranting and spins in my direction. I'm not laughing anymore. In fact, I'm not even breathing.

As he tries to locate the source of the sound—namely, me—his eyes narrow into a squint. He sinks into a stalking position, every muscle poised for pursuit. I still can't tell if he's seen me, but I'm starting to get scared. As he steps through the hole in the fence, I panic and take off.

He definitely sees me now. I don't need to look back to know he's chasing me—and catching up. I hear his footfalls on the path. We reach the sidewalk at the same time, and before I can make the turn onto the lane, he catches me in a bear hug. He's put on the brakes, but I'm

still moving forward, so, of course, we both lose our balance. If my momentum wins out, we will crash onto the sidewalk, but he's stronger and pulls me backward onto the grass. We still land with a thud though, and when my back slams into his chest, I hear the air rush out of him. He goes limp.

Now's my chance. I roll off him, but instead of scrambling to my feet and running, I hesitate. What if he's hurt?

Mistake. Before I can even check to see if he's alive, he grabs my wrists and tumbles me to the ground, pinning me down.

"You!" he shouts when he gets a look at my face. "Why are you spying on me?"

I squirm beneath the weight of his body, but it's no use. "Let me go!"

Still gripping my wrists, he eases himself up, but when I start kicking and writhing, he lowers himself right back down.

"Let me go!" I screech again.

"Only if you promise not to attack me." He grunts, trying to corral all my wriggling body parts.

I thought I was perspiring before, but that was nothing compared to the rivers of sweat running over me now. The guy is simply too strong. I have no more fight.

"Fine," I pant, letting my body go slack.

He doesn't release me.

"I said I give up!" I growl. "So get off me already."

"You're sure you're not going to kick me and take off again?"

"I'm sure. What do you want—a signed affidavit?" I scowl at him like I'm the one in control even though I'm pinned to the ground.

Eyeing me warily, he lets go of my wrists and pushes himself to his feet. Then he offers me a hand up.

I ignore his help and stand with as much dignity as I can muster. Then I brush the grass and dirt from my shorts and T-shirt, which are sticking to me like I've been swimming in them. My hair is plastered to my head, and sweat is dripping onto my neck. I'm sure I look lovely, but I'm too angry to care.

"I'll ask you one more time," he says, glaring at me. "Why were you spying on me?"

I fumble for a suitable excuse, but when nothing comes to mind, I opt for the truth. I prepare to run and scream, just in case. "I saw you go behind Greeley House during the ghost walk," I tell him. "The place is like a fortress, but you got in, no problem. I wanted to know how and why. So I came to find out."

"That's it?" He seems surprised.

I shrug. "You seemed to know an awful lot about the robberies that have

been going on." Saying my suspicions out loud makes them sound totally lame.

For a second he just frowns and blinks at me. Then his face breaks into a huge grin. "You thought I was the thief?" Without waiting for my answer, he bursts out laughing. "Seriously?" he manages between guffaws.

I bristle. "It's not that crazy. Somebody's the thief. Why not you? Holing up in a condemned house is exactly what a thief would do."

He stops laughing, and now it's his turn to shrug. "Okay, so your theory's not totally off-the-wall. But believe me, I am not the thief."

"So why were you sleeping in the house?"

"'Cause it beats sleeping on a park bench. I don't have money for a place. Okay?"

"But you have a job," I counter.

"Actually, I have two jobs. I lifeguard at the pool during the day and wait tables at a restaurant in the evenings. But I need every penny I earn."

"For what?" Now that he's on the defensive, I want to keep him there.

He scowls. "Not that it's any of your business, but I'm saving for a conference. I got a scholarship to an elite magicians' school, and part of it is held in Las Vegas. Some of the world's best magicians are putting this on. My classes are covered, but I still have to pay for my accommodations in Vancouver, my airfare to Vegas, my hotel and my food."

"A school for magicians?" I say. "You're a magician?"

He nods. "I'm trying to be."

"That still doesn't explain why you have no place to stay. Where's home? It's obviously not Witcombe."

"Calgary," he says. "Well, it used to be Calgary. But my dad wants me to study law and join his firm. I took one year at U of C, but it's not for me. I told him I want to be a magician—I've been doing magic since I was ten—but as far as he's concerned, that's not an option. It's his way or the highway." He shrugs again. "So I took the highway. I figured I'd work my way to Vancouver."

I glance back at Greeley House. "Looks like your hotel has gone out of business. So now what? Know any magic for conjuring free accommodation?"

He sighs. "I wish."

Chapter Six

The next day is much cooler. It's still warm, but not frying-pan hot like before. The streets are full of tourists again, and so is the antique shop. People aren't just browsing either. The merchandise is practically selling itself. This is a good thing, because although I like antiques, I don't know much about them. If customers want old doorknobs

or snow globes, I can steer them in the right direction. But if it's an antique boot scraper or nutmeg grater they're after—which one lady was searching for this morning—Aunt Maude has to help them.

My task is to keep customers happy while they wait. That's not generally too tough a job. Most people are on holiday, so they're in a good mood and are content to browse until Aunt Maude gets to them.

As I talk with the customers, I try to keep one eye on the front door, but even so, I don't see the Spence sisters come in. Not that it matters. They see me and head over to say hello. Again, they're dressed identically.

"Christine, isn't it?" one of them says. "You were on the ghost walk."

"Yes, I was." I smile. "And you are Agatha and Hilary. Just don't ask me to tell you which one's which."

They chuckle, and one of them crooks a finger for me to come close.

When I do, she whispers, "Truth is, we rather enjoy confusing people. That's one of the reasons we dress alike."

"Are you ladies looking for something specific today?" I ask.

"As a matter of fact, yes," they say in unison. One of them adds, "We have a lovely collection of loose-tea infusers, and we'd love to add to it."

"Loose-tea infusers?"

"Yes, yes," the other sister says. "You know—those hollow metal balls that hold tea leaves. They do the same job as tea bags, but they can be used over and over. Very environmentally friendly, aren't they, sister?"

Her twin nods. "Very. Do you have any?"

I nod. "I'm pretty sure we have a basket of them over this way. Follow me."

Once the Spence sisters start digging through the tea infusers, I return to the front of the store.

"Can I help you find something?" I ask a woman I pass on the way.

"Actually, I've already found too many things," she says as she juggles an armful of items. "What I need is to pay for them and leave this shop before I bankrupt myself."

We both laugh, and I relieve her of some of her load. "Well, let's get you to the cash register, then," I say and lead the way to the service counter. "That will be $237.53," I tell her when I've rung in the sale.

She hands me her credit card. I process it and hand it back along with the bag of purchases. "Thank you for shopping at Maude's Antiques, Mrs. Thatcher. Enjoy the rest of your day."

It seems all the shoppers are ready to pay at the same time, because suddenly there's a long line at the till. When Mrs. Thatcher returns twenty minutes later, I'm still ringing through purchases.

"Excuse me," she says as she slides in front of the woman next in line. "I'm sorry to interrupt. I promise I won't be a minute." Then she turns to me. "I don't know if you remember me, but I bought some postcards and some hand-painted things here a few minutes ago."

I nod. "Yes, Mrs. Thatcher. I remember you. Is there a problem?"

She bobs her head. "Yes, there is. I can't seem to find my wallet. Did I leave it here? It's navy blue. About this big." She draws it in the air. "I just tried to pay for something in another shop, and I didn't have it."

I make a thorough search of my side of the counter while she does the same on hers, and then we both check the floor. By this time, other customers are looking around as well.

"I'm sorry, Mrs. Thatcher," I tell her. "It isn't here."

Aunt Maude appears out of nowhere. "What seems to be the trouble?"

"This lady has lost her wallet," I say.

"I was sure I put it back in my purse." The woman is actually wringing her hands.

"I thought you did too," I say.

Aunt Maude offers Mrs. Thatcher a reassuring smile. "Perhaps if you retrace your steps," she suggests.

The woman frowns, trying to remember. "Well, on my way out, I—I stopped at the bureau over there to admire the antique hand mirrors. I only put my purse down for a few seconds. It couldn't have been any longer, I'm sure."

Aunt Maude searches the area around the bureau, but the wallet isn't there.

The shop becomes painfully quiet. I'm wracking my brain, trying to think where else to look, what else to do, how to placate Mrs. Thatcher. And then—

"It's the thief!" a customer cries out, and everyone turns. "You know—the guy who's been breaking into motels and picking people's pockets in all the towns around here. Quick, everyone, check to make sure you haven't been robbed too."

"Now, now…" Aunt Maude tries to keep a lid on things. But a wave of panic moves through the store, and people dig into their pockets and purses, hunting for their own wallets. "There's no need to panic. I'm sure there's a reasonable expla—"

She is cut off by one of the Spence sisters. "Oh no," she gasps, holding out her open purse. "My wallet is missing too."

While we wait for the police, Aunt Maude closes the shop and rings through the patrons' purchases, all the

while assuring them that Bill and Andy—Witcombe's local RCMP detachment—will get to the bottom of things. I'm in charge of serving iced tea. Considering that no one can leave until they've been questioned, Aunt Maude says it's the civilized thing to do.

I stand out of the way while the customers are questioned. One by one, they exit the shop. Finally, only Bill and Andy, the Spence sisters and Mrs. Thatcher are left. While the officers confer, Aunt Maude and I join the robbery victims to offer support.

Mrs. Thatcher cocks her head toward Agatha—she was the sister who was robbed—and says, "You look very familiar."

The sisters look at each other, and Agatha says, "Well, as you can see, I have a very common face."

Mrs. Thatcher frowns. "Yes, I see that you are twins, but…"

"What is it?" Aunt Maude prompts her when she pauses.

"Well, it's just that I'm sure I've seen this woman before."

"We've been in Witcombe almost a week," Agatha offers. "Perhaps you've seen us in a restaurant or another shop."

"Now I remember where it was," Mrs. Thatcher exclaims. "Out on the street when I left the shop. We bumped into each other."

The sisters exchange glances again.

"As I said, our face is pretty common." Agatha chuckles. "The older we get, the more we look like every other old lady out there. But I assure you, it wasn't me—or Hilary—you bumped into. I remember seeing you in the shop earlier and again when you returned, but Hilary and I were here that whole time."

"It's true, Mrs. Thatcher," I say. "I can vouch for them. They were both here all that time."

Mrs. Thatcher shakes her head. "You're right, of course. It must have been someone else. I guess I'm more upset about this robbery than I realize."

When Bill and Andy are satisfied that Agatha Spence and Mrs. Thatcher have nothing more to tell them, everyone leaves the shop. Aunt Maude locks the door and leaves the *CLOSED* sign in place.

"That's enough excitement for one day," she sighs, flopping down on an antique settee. "I was so sure Witcombe would be spared." She shakes her head. "Now I'm going to be watching everyone like a hawk. Anyone could be the thief."

Not quite anyone, I think. It couldn't be Simon the magician. He was never even in the shop.

Chapter Seven

For the rest of the afternoon, all I can think about is the robbery. Two people had their wallets stolen, and I didn't even notice. I try to figure out who looked suspicious. Nobody. Everybody! Which customers were looking at antiques, and which ones were stalking other customers? I have no idea. I've never had any encounters with crooks before.

The realization that I can't tell the good guys from the bad guys bothers me.

I think Aunt Maude might be feeling the same way. After she closes the shop, she goes to her bedroom and stays there until suppertime. She looks more tired when she comes out than she did when she went in.

"Did you sleep?" I say, looking up from the magazine I'm browsing.

She shakes her head. "No. I was too busy thinking. Lying down is good for that. But enough is enough. It's time to move on." She gestures for me to get up. "Come on, Christine. Run a comb through your hair, and I'll put on some lipstick. We're going out to dinner at Shep's."

Based on the name, I guess the restaurant will be a hole-in-the-wall diner run by a guy with greasy hair who cooks corned-beef hash while sucking on a cigarette.

I'm not even close.

Shep's might be the fanciest restaurant I've ever been to. It has classy decor, white linen, polished silver, sparkling glassware—even cushy carpeting.

When we walk in, there are about ten people waiting in the foyer. We don't have a reservation, so I think we'll be leaving on empty stomachs. But Aunt Maude marches up to the hostess like she owns the place. I don't hear what she says, but the hostess nods and smiles and picks up a couple of menus, and the next thing I know, we are following her to a table. It's small and in an out-of-the-way corner, but it's a table, and we didn't have to wait for it.

The hostess pours water and takes our drink order, a soft drink for me and a Harvey Wallbanger for Aunt Maude.

"Your server will be right with you," she says with a smile before leaving us.

"How'd you manage that?" I ask, taking a sip of my water. "There was a pile of people ahead of us."

She pushes her glasses up on her nose and opens the menu. "Sometimes who you know is more important than what you know. Shep D'Amico and I went to school together."

Everything on the menu sounds fabulous. I can't decide what to have. I still haven't made up my mind when our server arrives.

"What can I get for you ladies this evening?" he says.

I look up. It's Simon.

"Hi." I beam. "I didn't know you worked here."

"Hi yourself." He smiles back. "I told you I worked in a restaurant."

"Yeah, but you didn't say it was this one."

He shrugs.

I turn to Aunt Maude. "You remember Simon. He came in on the tail end of your ghost walk the other night."

Aunt Maude lets her glasses slide down her nose and squints at him over the top of them. "Ah, yes," she says finally. "The young man who gave us the news about the robberies in Kaleden."

That reminds me of today's thefts.

"Speaking of robberies, Simon, did you hear about the excitement at the antique shop this afternoon?"

He shakes his head.

"The thief struck again. Stole the wallets from two of our customers. The police were called in and questioned everyone in the store."

"Really?" Simon says. "Do they have any suspects?"

"If they do, they didn't tell us."

"It looks like nowhere is safe," he says. "Hang on to your purses, ladies.

I'd hate for you to have to wash dishes to pay for your supper." He grins. "So what can I get for you?"

When we've ordered and Simon turns to leave, I touch his arm and whisper, "Did you find somewhere to sleep last night?"

"Yeah. Another one of the waiters let me crash at his place. I can stay there for a couple more nights maybe, but I'm going to have to find something more permanent. If you hear of anything, let me know."

"What was that about?" Aunt Maude asks when he's gone. "Did he get evicted?"

I half smile. "You could say that." I explain how Simon was trying to save money by sleeping at Greeley House. "Whoever owns the place found out he was there. When he came back yesterday, his stuff was outside on the ground, and there was a shiny new padlock on the

door with a sign that said it was private property and that trespassers will be prosecuted."

Aunt Maude snorts and waves her hand. "Hogwash. Weren't either of you listening on the ghost walk? I said the town took over the property for back taxes. That house is no more private than the Fraser River. Someone's yanking Simon's chain—yours too. Your friend is nothing more than the victim of a practical joke. Not that the town would want anyone going into the old house. It's a death trap." She pauses and eyes me suspiciously. "When did you and Simon get so chummy?"

It's probably not a good idea to tell her that I suspected he was the thief and I was spying on him. And it's definitely not a good idea to tell her I went exploring in Greeley House. So I say, "Besides working here, Simon is a lifeguard at the pool."

Nothing like a little half-truth to get a person off the hook. Aunt Maude nods knowingly, mutters "Mm-hmm" and lets the subject drop.

Though we've come to the restaurant to get our minds off the thefts at the antique shop, I can't seem to chase them from my brain.

"Aunt Maude," I say, "I know you don't like the idea, but after what happened today, don't you think you should beef up the security at your shop?" I pause, waiting for her to balk. When all she does is take a sip of her Harvey Wallbanger, I keep talking. "The lock on the door is as old as the merchandise you sell. A six-year-old could pick it. You have no alarm system and no security cameras. You don't even lock the glass cabinets where the valuable items are kept."

"My customers don't know that," she says.

I roll my eyes. "That's not the point."

She puts her drink down. "Do you really think the thief would have the gall to strike again in the same place? He never has before."

"Which is exactly why he might. He's unpredictable. That's why the police can't catch him—or her," I add. "There's no reason why it couldn't be a woman. Equal opportunity and all that. Anyway, could you at least think about improving your security?"

"I *have* thought about it," Aunt Maude announces in a tone that means further argument is a waste of breath.

I sigh as Simon arrives with our food.

"Enjoy your meals," he says, "and if there's anything else you need, please let me know."

"Not so fast, young man," Aunt Maude says. "I understand you are without lodging."

Simon glares at me.

I glare right back. "You didn't say it was a secret." Man, you'd think I'd committed treason.

"Well?" Aunt Maude ropes him back in.

"Yes, ma'am." He nods.

"Then I have a proposition for you," she continues. "You are in need of a bed, and I am in need of a night watchman. My great-niece is concerned that my shop might be robbed. I have a suite of rooms above the store, but I'm a sound sleeper. So if someone breaks in during the night, I might not hear.

"I have a cot in the storage room of my shop, which I am offering you for the duration of your stay in Witcombe. In exchange, you will keep an ear out for burglars. I certainly don't expect you to stay awake. Just sleep lightly. There is a washroom, and I shall give you a key

to the rear entrance of the shop—if the arrangement suits you. What do you say?"

Simon looks at me. "Did you ask your aunt to do this?"

I shake my head. "It's news to me."

"Well?" Aunt Maude cuts in. "Yes or no? My dinner is getting cold."

Chapter Eight

Aunt Maude might think evicting Simon from Greeley House was a practical joke, but I'm not so sure. For one thing, Simon never told anyone he was staying there. Somebody would have had to follow him to find that out—and there was no reason to do that. I only staked out the place because I saw him sneak onto the property during the ghost walk.

And isn't the point of a practical joke to laugh in the face of the guy who's been tricked? Nobody's done that.

I might be jumping to conclusions, but I can't help thinking that whoever booted Simon out of Greeley House wanted the place for himself.

What I have to find out is *why*.

I start my investigation the next morning. Aunt Maude says she won't need me in the shop until the afternoon, so it's back to the old mansion after breakfast. That's the only lead I have. I hope someone shows up. I'm probably wasting my time, but you never know. Like my mom always says—nothing ventured, nothing gained.

So much for old adages. I arrive at the mansion at 8:00 AM, and three hours later, all I have to show for the morning are cramped legs and a bursting bladder. Stakeouts look exciting on television, but in real life they're just plain boring.

At least I have my phone to entertain me this time. I'm ready to throw in the private-investigator towel when a zebra turns off the sidewalk and starts up the trail beside the wrought-iron fence.

Okay, so it's not really a zebra, but when I see black-and-white stripes moving through a wall of green, that's my first thought. Unless we're in Africa, this is not camouflage.

Even from a distance, I can tell it's a woman. Judging from the white hair and the slowness of her step, it's an old woman. So right away I'm thrown off. What is an old lady doing at a run-down house on an abandoned street?

As she gets closer, I blink to make sure I'm really seeing what I'm seeing. It's one of the Spence sisters. What's *she* doing here? And where's the other one? I peer past her toward the sidewalk. There's no such thing as one twin. Hilary and Agatha might as well

be joined at the hip. They do everything together.

Apparently, not this time.

So now I'm more than curious. My immediate impulse is to jump up and confront her, but I force myself to stay in hiding and watch.

She may not have sprinted up the path, but Agatha—or Hilary—isn't the least bit winded when she gets to the top. For an old woman, she's in pretty good shape. Without pausing, she goes directly to the fence, takes out the removable bar and steps through. *Does everybody in Witcombe know about this secret entrance?* Then she replaces the bar and heads directly to the hedge.

Once she's around it, I can't see her anymore, but I hear the rattle of the padlock and the unmistakable scraping of the door on the stones.

I'm totally baffled. Obviously, the Spence sisters put the lock on the door

and posted the *KEEP OUT* notice—
which they had no right to do. So what
do they want with the old place?

The only way I'm going to find out
is to follow this twin.

That is easier said than done. I wait
almost an hour for her to come outside,
but she doesn't. I'm tempted to sneak
up to the window of the only accessible
room and try to look inside, but I don't
dare. With my luck, she'll be staring
right back at me or she'll exit the house
while I'm creeping past the door.

I check my phone for the time. It's
noon. I can't hang around much longer.
I promised Aunt Maude I'd be at the
shop by 1:00. What could the Spence
twin be doing in there so long?

I have another thought. What if she
isn't inside anymore? Maybe there's
another exit that I don't know about.
I can't think where it could be, but that

doesn't mean there isn't one. If there's a secret entrance through the fence, there could very well be a secret exit from the house.

I wait another fifteen minutes, but she still doesn't show. I have to leave. It will take me twenty minutes to walk to the shop. That leaves me less than a half hour to make lunch and eat.

Because I'm in a hurry, the Witcombe streets are a postcard of life in slow motion. I swerve around the window-shoppers like a slalom skier maneuvering the gates. As I veer to miss a woman pushing a stroller, I almost crash into a low wall surrounding the patio of a restaurant. On the other side, at a table not three feet away, is a pair of zebras.

They look up from their lunch and smile.

"Hello, Christine. Shopping?" one of them says.

"Or are you here for lunch too?" asks the other. "This is a fabulous little bistro. I highly recommend it."

I can't believe my eyes. This is not possible. I just left one of these old ladies at Greeley House, yet here they both are in downtown Witcombe. There's no way the twin at the mansion could have left after me and beat me back to town.

Unless she had a car. Or unless she left by another exit.

I squelch my surprise and bewilderment and force my face into what I hope is a smile.

"Neither," I say. "I'm supposed to help out at the antique shop this afternoon— Aunt Maude has an appointment—but I lost track of the time. If I don't hurry, I'll be late." At this point, I should wave goodbye and start running again, but I'm too curious to leave. "So how did you ladies spend the morning?" I ask.

"We took a tour of the Miners' Museum. The guide was a lovely woman whose great-grandfather survived that terrible cave-in back in the early 1900s," says one.

The other sister nods. "We also met a young couple from Missouri who are honeymooning here. Most newlyweds go someplace tropical, but Perry and Jenna—that's the young couple—decided to tour the Okanagan instead. Apparently, Perry's grandmother is from British Columbia. Such a sweet young pair, weren't they, Agatha?"

"Yes, indeed. We have met so many wonderful people during our trip. I shall be sad for it to end. But only two more days and it will be over."

Agatha frowns. "I shan't miss all those robberies though."

I jump on the change of subject. "Speaking of robberies, have you heard

from the police? Have they found your wallet? Do they have any leads?"

Agatha shakes her head. "No leads that we know of, but then, how could we? The police haven't been in touch. I imagine they're busy investigating the latest theft."

"There's been another one?"

Hilary nods. "Yes. Just this morning. A man had his pocket picked in a shopping mall in Summerland."

The Spence sisters continue to talk, and I continue to smile and nod, but I'm not listening anymore. I'm trying to figure out how an old lady beat me back to town.

"Do you have a car?" I blurt.

They both look at me strangely.

"Why, yes. We rented one at the airport in Kelowna. Why do you ask, dear?"

Other than telling them I suspect they might be involved with the robberies,

I don't have an answer. I shrug. "It looks like it's going to be hot again this afternoon. I'd hate for you to have to walk back to your cottage."

They smile, and one of them says, "Actually, the car is at the service station. We dropped it there this morning. It was backfiring." She holds up her cell phone. "The mechanic just called. One of the spark-plug connections was loose. But it's all fixed now. We can pick it up as soon as we finish our lunch."

I smile and nod. "Good. I'd hate for you to get sunstroke. It's been nice chatting with you, but I have to go. Aunt Maude will be waiting for me."

Chapter Nine

So much for my theory about the twin I saw at Greeley House driving back to town. If her car was at a service station, she couldn't have. She had to have left by some other exit. There's only one way to find out.

I have just enough time to go back to the mansion. But I don't want the Spence twins knowing what I'm doing,

so I run a half-block toward the antique shop before I cross the street and double back. Then I bolt to the mansion like an Olympic runner.

I let myself through the fence and move across the grass to the house. Then I peek around the hedge at the door.

The padlock is back in place. *Darn!* Growling in frustration, I stalk to the door and give the lock a good tug, in case it's unlocked. It isn't. Well, that proves it—the twin I saw had to have left after I did.

I frown and scratch my head. So how did she beat me back to town? None of this makes any sense.

In detective shows, solving crimes looks like a snap. All of the puzzle pieces fall neatly into place, and the bad guys get caught. Either those TV shows are a huge lie, or I'm really bad at this.

The thing is, I shouldn't be. I'm pretty observant and good at gathering clues.

The problem is, I suck at putting the evidence together and coming up with the *correct* conclusions.

For instance, I saw Simon sneak into Greeley House. I saw him leave it again the next day. I discovered all his stuff in the mansion like he was living there. Normal people don't live in ramshackle, abandoned buildings. But thieves very well might. Conclusion: Simon was the robber.

Totally logical—and totally wrong. It never occurred to me that Simon might have other reasons for staying in Greeley House. I wanted him to be the robber, so I put the evidence together so that it looked like he was. No wonder he laughed his head off when I accused him of being the crook.

Right then and there, I should have given up sleuthing, but of course I didn't. I must be a glutton for punishment. No, I see the lock on the door

and the *NO TRESPASSING* sign, and I poke my nose into things all over again. The thing is, I'm no better at it this time around than I was before.

The only difference is that now I think the Spence sisters are the thieves—even though there's no way they could be. When the people were being robbed in Kaleden, the twins were on the ghost walk in Witcombe. During this morning's robbery, they were visiting a local museum with a pile of other people. The only time they were at the scene of one of the robberies was at the antique store, but that time Agatha Spence was one of the victims. Who robs themselves?

"Give it up, Christine," I scold myself aloud. "The twins are *not* the thieves."

There has to be a logical reason for one of them being here this morning and having a key to the locked door. There's also got to be an explanation for how she got back to town so fast.

Maybe the little room with the window will tell me something. I hurry across the yard. Cupping my hands around my eyes to cut out the glare of the sun, I press my face against the glass.

All I see is total darkness. I can't even make out shadows. I pull away from the window and immediately realize what the problem is. Someone has covered the inside of the window with black paper. Obviously, Agatha—or Hilary—doesn't want me seeing what's inside. Why? What are they hiding?

"Nothing!" I yell to the air. "Nothing, nothing, nothing." But it doesn't matter how many times I say it, I can't make myself believe it.

I check the time. *Yikes!* It's 12:40. I only have twenty minutes to get to the antique shop. I call Aunt Maude to let her know I'm on my way, and then I race back to town.

Chapter Ten

I'm thinking maybe I should bounce my theory off someone who's not involved. My mind automatically goes to Simon. He knows about Greeley House and my interest in the robberies. But he's objective. If my ideas are totally out to lunch, he'll tell me. He'll remind me that the thief or thieves don't have to be hiding out in Witcombe. Since the robberies

have occurred all over the Okanagan Valley, the crook could be staying anywhere. The thief might actually *live* in the Okanagan and have a home here— even a job! Also, he'll tell me that if he'd had a good reason for holing up in Greeley House, the Spence sisters probably do too. Besides, they're not living in the mansion. They're staying in a cottage. All I know for sure is that they have a key for the padlock. Just because I saw one of them go inside doesn't mean she's hiding stolen goods. Maybe the place is for sale and a realtor gave her the key to the padlock so she could look around.

I smile to myself. Just by trying to think like Simon, I've come up with a pile of explanations for what I've seen, and none of them point to a crime. Clearly, I've been letting my imagination run away with me.

By the time I arrive at the antique shop, I'm pretty much thinking like

a normal person again. This is a good thing, because Simon isn't there to talk sense into me. Aunt Maude says he came by to drop off his stuff and collect the door key, but then he went to work. I'm disappointed. Even though I've almost talked myself out of my crime theories, I still want to find out what Simon thinks. After his shift at the pool, he shows up to change his clothes but zooms away again to his restaurant job.

"I'm off at 11:00," he says. "We can talk then."

The evening drags by. I stare at the television, but I don't register what I'm watching. I play Scrabble with Aunt Maude, but the longest word I put down is *cat*.

"This is a waste of time," she finally says, wiping the tiles off the board with a sweep of her arm. "The goldfish is

more competition than you. Where's your head tonight, girl? It certainly isn't here."

I shrug. There's no way I'm telling her I'm counting the minutes until I can talk with Simon. She'll think there's something romantic between us. And if she thinks that, she might un-invite him to be her night watchman.

"It's just one of those days," I say. I stand and push in my chair. "I'm sorry. I know I'm not very good company. I may as well go to bed. Goodnight, Aunt Maude." I squeeze her shoulder and kiss the top of her head.

She pats my hand. "Goodnight, Christine. I think I'll hit the hay too. At my age, you can't get too much beauty sleep. Tomorrow is another day. What do you say we start it off with a big breakfast?"

"Pizza?" I tease.

"Actually, I was thinking spaghetti and meatballs with garlic toast." She winks.

She's teasing—I think. I give her shoulder another squeeze. "Even better. See you in the morning."

After cleaning my teeth and washing my face, I crawl under the covers with my clothes on. There's no way I'm letting Simon see me in my pajamas. On the other hand, if Aunt Maude comes into my room, I don't want her asking why I'm still in my clothes.

I peer at the clock beside the bed. It's 10:30. Simon won't be back for a while. Until then, I have to make sure I stay awake—and hope Aunt Maude falls asleep.

No worries on that front. Before I know it, she's snoring. When I hear the back door of the shop clicking shut, I look at the clock again. It's 11:15.

Grabbing the mini-flashlight from the night table, I throw back the covers, tiptoe to the door and open it. Aunt Maude is still snoring. I slip into the hall and quietly make my way down to the antique shop. The blinds are closed, so except for a crack of light under the door of the storeroom, the shop is in darkness. I aim the flashlight beam at the floor and follow the dim path it creates.

Simon opens the door before I can knock. It happens so quickly and unexpectedly that I scream—sort of. It's actually more of a squeak, but Simon yanks me into the storeroom and closes the door.

"Ssshhhh. You'll wake your aunt."

"You scared me!" I say in my defense.

"Sorry. Have a seat." He gestures toward the cot.

I look around for a chair. There isn't one. The idea of sitting on Simon's bed

feels weird—I mean, the guy is totally hot. But there are no other options, so I sit.

"What do you want to talk to me about?"

I've been waiting all day to get Simon's take on things, but now that the moment has arrived, I'm embarrassed to tell him about my sleuthing.

"Promise you won't laugh."

He shakes his head. "No."

"What do you mean, *no*?"

"If it's funny, I'll probably laugh. I like laughing. Why would I promise not to?"

I wrinkle my nose at him. "Thanks a lot. You're not making this easy, you know."

He sighs. "Okay, fine. You want easy? How about this? You've found a new suspect for the Okanagan robberies."

My jaw literally drops open. "How can you know that?"

He waggles his eyebrows. "Magic."

I swat him. "No. Seriously. Why would you say that?"

"Think about it, Christine. You and I hardly know each other. I saw you on the ghost walk and at the pool. I served you at the restaurant. What is the one thing we have in common?" He doesn't even give me a chance to answer. "Greeley House and the robberies. And since you were staking the place out before, I'm guessing you've been at it again. And now you think you know who the thief is." He pauses. "Am I close?"

I scowl and nod. "And you think I'm being dumb."

He shakes his head and puts up his hands. "I never said that. Like you said before—somebody's gotta be the thief. Your theories are as good as anyone else's. The police sure haven't solved the case. So now that I'm off your hit list—I am off it, right?"

When I offer him an unamused sneer, he smiles and continues. "So who do you think the crook is?"

"The Spence sisters," I say and wait for Simon to split a gut laughing.

He doesn't. "Those twin old ladies who were on the ghost walk?"

I nod.

"What makes you suspect *them*?"

"Because one of them has a key for the padlock on Greeley House."

"How do you know that?"

"I saw her use it to get in today."

"Really? That *is* interesting."

"Interesting, yes, but it doesn't prove anything." I tell him about the twin beating me back to town. Then I outline all the other holes in my theory. "And the Spence sisters have an alibi for every robbery. They are always somewhere else with a ton of witnesses."

Instead of agreeing with me, Simon says, "That in itself is suspicious."

"Why?"

"The first law of magic is that things are not what they seem. A magician draws people's eyes away from what he's doing. He makes them see what he wants them to see. The mind jumps to conclusions by the power of suggestion. The twins told you their car was at the service station, but was it? Maybe the one twin did know of another exit from Greeley House. Maybe Agatha wasn't robbed. Maybe she only said she was to draw suspicion away from herself."

"You think?"

"Sure, why not? I think the twins wanted to be noticed at other places so no one would suspect them. But people aren't watching them the whole time. They stand out when they want to be noticed—like wearing the zebra-stripe dresses, and they blend in when they want to be inconspicuous. You may have thought they were on the ghost walk

the whole time, but maybe one of them disappeared for a while and you didn't notice."

"I don't know, Simon. It seems like a stretch to me. Not that it matters. Either way, we'll know in a couple of days."

"How's that?"

"That's when they're heading home. They told me today. If they leave and the robberies stop, we'll know it was them. If the robberies continue, they're innocent."

Simon's face breaks into a grin. "Unless we catch them in the act before then."

I frown. "And how are we going to manage that?"

That's when the storeroom door swings open and Aunt Maude says, "Precisely what I was wondering."

Chapter Eleven

It's midnight. Aunt Maude and I sit in darkness, staring out my bedroom window at the street below. The shops are closed, and the sidewalks that bustled with people during the day are empty. It's dark except for a few puddles of light cast by ancient street-lights. Witcombe is asleep.

We can see the other side of the street, but anyone who might be walking on our side is hidden. Simon, on guard in the shop below, will be the first to know if someone tries to break in. But Aunt Maude and I watch anyway.

"Do you think the twins will take the bait?" I whisper.

"I guess it depends on how convincing our performance was this afternoon *and* if they're the thieves," Aunt Maude replies.

I feel a grin creep across my face. "Oscar nominations in our future for sure."

Aunt Maude chuckles. "I don't know about that, but it was certainly fun. I'm sorry my exit came so early in the scene. I would have liked to see the sisters' reaction."

"When you stormed out of the restaurant, they were hooked. All I had to do was reel them in."

"So what happened after I left?"

"Well, I pretended to be really upset. I wiped the corner of my eye, sniffed a little, blinked back tears and tried not to look at anyone. I bit my lip too. I wanted to look like I needed comforting."

"I hope you didn't overdo it."

I shake my head. "Not a chance. The sisters were so curious, they couldn't stay in their seats. Almost right away, they scurried over to me. They consoled me for a few minutes and then encouraged me to explain what had caused the argument between you and me."

"What did you say?"

"The truth."

Even in the dark, I can tell Aunt Maude is bristling.

"Kidding." I laugh and give her a peck on the cheek. "But I did use our past discussions about security as inspiration. I just amped them up a bit."

"Details, please, Christine."

"I told them how the shop had no night lighting, no security system and no surveillance cameras. I said I was especially concerned now that there have been so many thefts in the area, but that you refuse to listen to reason. You are stubbornly resisting taking proper security precautions. Then I lowered my voice and confided that just today you brought in a violin worth $50,000 for a local collector. I told them that he's out of town right now, and you have to keep it at the shop in a safe that doesn't even lock!

"You should have seen their faces and heard their gasps when I put that one out there.

"Then I dangled the biggest carrot of all right under their noses. I said the lock on the shop's front door was faulty. I told them that I had tried to prove to you how useless it was by breaking into the shop using a piece of wire. But not even that would convince you."

"What did they say to that?"

"There was more gasping and tut-tutting. They patted my back a few more times and told me not to let the situation upset me. They were sure you'd come to your senses. Then they excused themselves and left the restaurant. They didn't even finish their lunch."

"Well," and Aunt Maude heaves a huge sigh, "if they're the thieves, I think you've given them incentive to strike again."

"Do *you* think they're the robbers?"

"Honestly?" she says. "I don't know. I have to admit that they intentionally draw attention to themselves, and that is a bit odd. But there have been so many robberies, I don't see how they could have committed all of them."

I nod. "I know what you mean. But even so, I still think they're the crooks. Tonight will tell. The thieves usually lift people's wallets, but they seem to be experts at breaking and entering too.

And the antique shop is a ripe Okanagan peach just waiting to be picked. How can they resist?"

Aunt Maude rubs her hands together gleefully. "Well, it's a clever plan regardless. I haven't had this much fun since I tricked snooty Betty Smith into wolfing down a dog-food sandwich."

I shouldn't be surprised, but I am. "You made someone eat a dog-food sandwich?"

"Well, I didn't force-feed her, if that's what you're thinking. She ate it voluntarily. Of course, she didn't know it was dog food until she was chewing the last bite."

"Aunt Maude!" I exclaim. "That's terrible."

She shrugs. "Betty thought so too. She spent the next fifteen minutes in the bathroom, throwing up."

I shake my head, but I'm smiling. My great-aunt is one crazy lady.

"So what made you come downstairs last night?" I ask. "Did you hear me squeal?"

"I was only five feet behind you, so it was pretty hard to miss."

"But you were sleeping," I protest. "I heard you snoring."

She peers at me over the top of her glasses. "I was snoring to make you think I was sleeping. I knew you were up to something."

"How?" I demand indignantly.

"You're not the only one who's a detective, you know," she scoffs. "You ran into the shop yesterday afternoon looking for Simon, and the rest of the day you were distracted. It was obvious that whatever had you distracted had something to do with him. When you went to bed early, I was sure of it. A late-evening liaison was in the wind. So I went along with the game.

I pretended to be asleep and followed you downstairs. Then I listened at the door."

"That's eavesdropping!"

She shrugs. "I call it investigative supervision."

"What if we'd been, you know, kissing or something?"

"Oh, please." She waves away my objection. "He's not your type."

"How do you know what my—" My question is interrupted by the vibration of my phone in my pocket.

There's a text from Simon. My heart skips a beat. I read it quickly and put my hand on Aunt Maude's arm.

Then I lift a finger to my lips and whisper, "It's happening."

Chapter Twelve

"Someone's trying to break in?" Aunt Maude gasps. "Really? You're serious?"

"Really," I tell her. "Right now. Simon says someone picked the lock on the front door faster than you can open it with the key. Time to call the police."

I dial 9-1-1, and whispering into Aunt Maude's phone, I explain the situation

and provide the address. "Yes, there's a robbery in progress right this minute."

"What is your location?"

"Maude's Antiques, 561 Main Street in Witcombe."

"Is the intruder armed?"

"I don't know."

"What is your name, please?"

"Christine Dowler. My great-aunt owns the shop. She's with me right now. I'm calling from the apartment above the shop."

"Are either of you hurt?"

"No. We're fine, but a friend is hiding in the shop downstairs, watching everything that's happening."

"Your friend's name?"

"Simon Rasmussen."

"Is he in immediate danger?"

"No. He's hiding in a storage room."

"Stay where you are. Do not confront the intruder. Officers are on their way."

"Hurry, please."

I turn off the phone. I don't want to take the chance of it ringing. It might scare away the burglar.

Aunt Maude and I grab each other's hands.

"Now what do we do?" she says.

"Wait for the police, I guess." I bite my lip. "I'm worried about Simon. It wouldn't be good if the thief discovered him."

Now that our trap has been sprung, it seems much less like a game. If the burglar has a weapon, Simon could be in real danger. The thief is undoubtedly one of the Spence sisters. The twins look and act like sweet little old ladies, but they're criminals, and it's not unusual for criminals to carry guns. I say a silent prayer for the police to hurry up and for Simon to stay in hiding.

I scan the road outside, hoping to see the flashing lights of police cars.

But there's nothing. I strain to catch sounds from the shop below. Nothing there either.

"I can't do this," I say. "I can't stay up here when something horrible could be happening downstairs."

Aunt Maude grips my arm fiercely. "Well, you can't go downstairs. The thief will see you for sure."

"You're right. You're right." I am trying to stay calm and slow my thoughts—which are currently flying through my head at warp speed. "I can't. It would wreck everything. But I can *look* downstairs."

"What do you mean, *look*?" Aunt Maude asks suspiciously.

"If I lie on the floor at the top of the stairs, I can see down into the shop. Then if Simon needs me, I'll be ready."

"Oh, I don't know, Christine. I'm pretty sure your mother wouldn't like this."

I screw up my face in disbelief. "What are you talking about? You've never cared whether or not Mom approves."

"That's true," she admits. "But I thought I should say something responsible. You can go—as long as you swear you'll stay at the top of the stairs."

As Aunt Maude releases her iron grip on my arm, the tension leaves my body.

"But I'm going too," she says.

"You can't!" I shake my head vehemently. "It means lying on the floor, Aunt Maude. If we have to get up in a hurry, you'll be toast."

She sniffs. "Just because I have a few miles on me doesn't mean I'm decrepit, my girl. Tomorrow we'll have a push-up competition, and then we'll see who the old lady is. Now stop arguing and let's go."

We take off our shoes and let ourselves into the hall. It's pitch black, but we've been sitting in the dark for

over an hour, so our eyes have adjusted. Just the same, we use the wall to guide us. As we near the stairs, we catch the glow of a flashlight.

There is no wall between the shop below and the stairs. They run parallel to the service counter and descend behind it. The burglar is heading straight toward them. There is no doubt the burglar is a woman. Her size and the way she moves give her away. Not that I can identify her. She's dressed entirely in black—including the balaclava covering her head.

For a second I think she's actually going to come upstairs. Talk about heart failure! All she has to do is direct the beam of her flashlight to the left, and we'll be right in her sights. Aunt Maude and I stay pinned to the wall until she moves soundlessly behind the service counter. As I expect, she heads straight for the safe.

Aunt Maude and I lower ourselves quietly to our knees and then down onto our stomachs. We have to inch forward a bit to see around the wall and look down at the service counter.

The thief tugs open the door of the safe and flashes her light inside. By the agitated way the beam jumps from the inside of the safe to the surrounding shelves, it's clear she doesn't see a violin. Now that she knows she's been duped, I expect her to cut her losses and make a run for it, but instead, she starts searching the rest of the shop.

Then I have a scary thought. What if she decides we took the violin upstairs for the night? No sooner do I think that than she turns around and starts for the stairs.

"Get up, Aunt Maude!" I whisper urgently. "She's coming up here!"

The words are barely out of my mouth when a siren wails, and a police car screeches to a halt in front of the store.

I see its flashing blue and red lights right through the blinds. The cavalry has arrived.

The woman stops, but as soon as a policeman—Bill, I think—bursts through the front door, she bolts for the back. I know I should stay where I am, but I can't let her get away, so I tear down the stairs. I get to the bottom just as she hauls open the back door and almost barrels into another policeman—Andy. Bill strides quickly across the shop and cuffs her hands behind her back.

It's over. I collapse against the wall as Simon switches on the lights and Aunt Maude makes her way down the stairs. Bill and Andy turn the burglar around and start leading her to the front of the store. The trio stops at the stairs, and Andy pulls the balaclava from the woman's head.

"Do you folks know this lady?" he says.

It's clearly one of the twins, but again, I have no idea which one.

"Agatha?" Aunt Maude makes a guess.

The woman shakes her head.

"Hilary then."

The woman smiles. "Neither, actually. I'm Esther. How do you do?"

As Simon, Aunt Maude and I sit down to breakfast the next morning, we're still shaking our heads.

"Triplets," Aunt Maude says for at least the twentieth time. It's strange enough seeing identical twins—but identical triplets? I still can't get my head around it. But it explains so much. I really should have been suspicious when Mrs. Thatcher said she thought she had run into Agatha in the street. It was Esther she'd bumped into, and that's when she'd had her wallet stolen.

But the robbery happened so close to where the other two sisters were that it compromised their alibi. So Agatha said she'd also been robbed in order to throw the police off the scent. That was pretty quick thinking.

"I know what the sisters did was against the law, but part of me can't help admiring them. While Esther was picking pockets and breaking into motel rooms and cottages, Hilary and Agatha were creating the perfect alibi. Nobody would ever suspect little old ladies of running a crime ring."

"*I* suspected them," I mumble through a mouthful of toast.

"You just got lucky." Simon laughs. "You suspected me too. Remember? And anyway, it was my master plan that flushed them out."

"But it wouldn't have worked if I wasn't such a convincing actress," I retort.

"Oh, for goodness' sake. Stop squabbling right now, both of you," Aunt Maude scolds. "We were all wonderful. And now that the police have collected the loot the sisters hid at Greeley House, the triplets are off to jail."

"I wouldn't be surprised if they've been pulling this scam all across Canada," I say.

Aunt Maude drops more bread into the toaster. "Well, I hope all the victims get their money back. I'm sure they'll all be more careful in the future. I know I will be. I've already made an appointment with a security company to set up an alarm system in the shop and get a new lock set."

"That's great!" I say and give her a high five.

Simon frowns. "Does that mean you won't need my services anymore, then?"

Aunt Maude winks at me and smiles at Simon. "Certainly not. The best security

system in the world is no substitute for a good night watchman—especially one who knows magic."

Kristin Butcher's other Orca Currents titles have been on recommended-reading lists such as the PSLA Top 40 (*Cheat*) and the YA Quick Picks nominee list (*Caching In*). Kristin lives in Campbell River, British Columbia. For more information, visit www.kristinbutcher.com.

orca *currents*

For more information on all the books
in the Orca Currents series, please visit
www.orcabook.com.